Country File
India

Lizann Flatt

Smart Apple Media

First published in 2001 by Franklin Watts
96 Leonard Street, London EC2A 4XD, UK

Franklin Watts Australia
56 O'Riordan Street, Alexandria, NSW 2015

Country File: India produced for Franklin Watts by
Bender Richardson White, PO Box 266, Uxbridge, UK.

Project Editor: Lionel Bender, Text Editor: Peter
Harrison, Designer: Ben White, Picture Researcher:
Cathy Stastny, Media Conversion and Make-up:
Mike Pilley/Radius, Production: Kim Richardson
Graphics: Mike Pilley/Radius, Maps: Stefan Chabluk
Copyright © 2001 Bender Richardson White

For Franklin Watts, Series Editor: Adrian Cole, Art
Director: Jonathan Hair

Published in the United States by Smart Apple Media
1980 Lookout Drive, North Mankato, MN 56003

Library of Congress Cataloging-in-Publication Data

Flatt, Lizann.
India / by Lizann Flatt.
p. cm. — (Country files)
Includes index.
Summary: An introduction to the geography,
government, economy, people, and culture of India.
ISBN 1-58340-201-2
1. India—Juvenile literature. [1. India.] I. Title.
II. Series.

DS407 .F56 2002
954—dc21   2002017030

9 8 7 6 5 4 3 2 1

Picture Credits

Pages: 1: PhotoDisc Inc./Glen Allison. 3: PhotoDisc
Inc./Santokh Kochar. 4: Hutchison Photo Library/David
Culverd. 7: PhotoDisc Inc./Santokh Kochar. 8: Hutchison
Photo Library/Jeremy Horner. 9: Hutchison Photo
Library/Juliet Highet. 10: PhotoDisc Inc./Santokh Kochar.
10–11: Hutchison Photo Library. 12 top: Hutchison Photo
Library/Jeremy Horner. 12–13 bottom: Hutchison Photo
Library/Nigara Film Workshop. 15 and 16: Hutchison
Photo Library/Jeremy Horner. 18: Hutchison Photo
Library/Liba Taylor. 19: Hutchison Photo Library/Nancy
Durrell McKenna. 20: Eye Ubiquitous/David Cumming.
21: Yann Arthus-Bertrand/CORBIS Pictures. 22 top:
Hutchison Photo Library/M. Jelliffe. 22 bottom: Hutchison
Photo Library. 24: Hutchison Photo Library/Maurice
Harvey. 25: Hutchison Photo Library. 26 top: Hutchison
Photo Library/Jeremy Horner. 26 bottom: James Davis
Travel Photography/James Davis. 28–29: PhotoDisc
Inc./Ingo Jezierski. 30: PhotoDisc Inc./Santokh Kochar.
31: PhotoDisc Inc./Ingo Jezierski.
Cover photo: James Davis Travel Photography.

The Author
Lizann Flatt is an award-winning author
and editor of children's nonfiction books
and magazines.

Contents

Welcome to India

The Republic of India, or Bharat as it is known to its people, is the second most populous country in the world. Roughly diamond-shaped, it is located in the northern hemisphere in south Asia.

In addition to the land on the Asian continent, India includes the Andaman and Nicobar Islands to the east and the Lakshadweep Islands to the west. Its total land area is roughly equal to one-third that of the United States.

A land full of contrasts and variety

The north of India is rimmed by the tallest mountain range in the world, the Himalayas, while the rest of the mainland is surrounded by water. India is known for its large population, rich religious and cultural heritage, many temples and holy sites, wildlife, textiles, tea plantations, and diamonds. It is a land where large cities and tribal villages, wealth and poverty, exist side by side.

DATABASE

Regions and Neighbors

Politically, India is a union of 28 states and seven territories that shares its northern borders with Pakistan, China, Nepal, Bhutan, Myanmar, and Bangladesh. Some of these borders are disputed, and occasionally military conflicts flare up between India and its neighbors.

At Dal Lake in Kashmir, northern India, boats are lined up awaiting tourist passengers. Kashmir is in the heart of the Himalaya region. ▼

The Land

Animals and Plants

India has a wide variety of habitats, or living areas, for animals and plants. These include mountains, rivers, forests, plains, and deserts. It therefore has a wide variety of Asian animals and plants.

Mammals:
Asiatic lions (only in national parks), leopards, tigers, Indian elephants, Indian rhinoceroses, deer, antelope, Asiatic wild buffalo (or water buffalo), yaks (mostly domesticated), Indian bison (or gaur), hyenas, jackals, giant flying squirrels, monkeys, bats, bears, and Gangetic dolphins.

Birds:
myna birds, peafowl (or peacocks), vultures, crows, pigeons, cranes, and storks.

Reptiles:
pythons, cobras, geckos, monitor lizards, and crocodiles.

Plants:
palm, laurel, maple, birch, conifer, ebony, teak, sandalwood, and banyan trees, grasses, bamboo, rhododendrons, and fruit trees such as mango, jackfruit, papaya, and banana.

India can be divided into three main geographical regions: the Himalaya Mountains, the Indo-Gangetic Plain, and the peninsula. There are large areas that can be farmed for food.

The Himalaya Mountains are covered with snow and ice, but rice paddies, orchards, forests, and tropical plants all grow in the valleys. Himalaya means "the land of snow," and it is the melting snow from these mountain tops that creates the three big rivers of the Gangetic Plain.

From farmland to desert

The Indo-Gangetic Plain is the main agricultural area of India. It is a flat, fertile area of cultivated farmland, but areas of deciduous trees and tuft grasses can be found. The region is crossed by the Indus, Ganges, and Brahmaputra Rivers. This is the most populated part of India, with such cities as New Delhi, Kanpur, and Varanasi. But it also contains the driest area, the Great Indian Desert in the west, where only scrub vegetation grows.

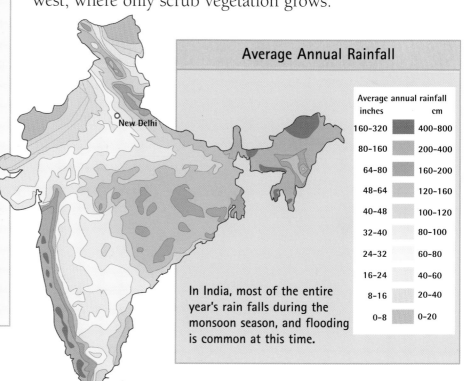

Average Annual Rainfall

New Delhi

Average annual rainfall	
inches	cm
160–320	400–800
80–160	200–400
64–80	160–200
48–64	120–160
40–48	100–120
32–40	80–100
24–32	60–80
16–24	40–60
8–16	20–40
0–8	0–20

In India, most of the entire year's rain falls during the monsoon season, and flooding is common at this time.

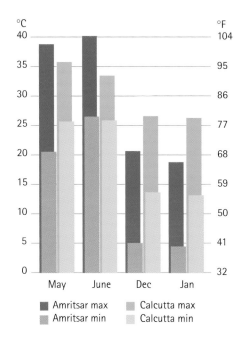

A distant view of the city of Pushkar in Rajasthan, northwest India. The city lies on the southern edge of the Great Indian Desert.

Maximum and minimum temperatures for Calcutta and Amritsar.

Southern mountains

The third region, the peninsula, is dominated by the Deccan Plateau, an area that contains some of the world's oldest rocks. The peninsula has its own river systems. Two mountain ranges, the Western Ghats and the Eastern Ghats, run close to the coast down the southern point of India. Deciduous and scrub forests grow in this region, and the Western Ghats contain tropical deciduous forests.

Climate

India has three major seasons: winter (November to March), summer (April to June), and the monsoon (June or July to October). During the monsoon season, it usually rains at least once a day in most places.

°C					°F
40					104
35					95
30					86
25					77
20					68
15					59
10					50
5					41
0	May	June	Dec	Jan	32

- ■ Amritsar max
- ■ Amritsar min
- ■ Calcutta max
- ■ Calcutta min

The People

India is the second most populous country in the world after China. It has ancient cultures, such as the Indus Valley and Dravidian traditions, which date back more than 4,500 years. The country's population is now estimated to be just over one billion and is still growing.

Over its long history, India has been settled or invaded by many different peoples. Each of these gradually merged with the existing populations, creating the diverse cultures and languages of today.

The Indian population has historically been divided into Indo-Aryans (people who migrated to India from the north), Dravidians (the original people from southern India), Mongoloids (people from the Himalaya mountains), and smaller groups.

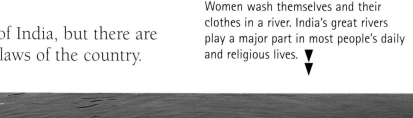

Female   Male

48%   52%

▲ There are far more men than women in India's population.

A mix of languages

Hindi is the national language of India, but there are 18 official languages listed in the laws of the country. There are also several hundred dialects listed by the census of India, but they can all be grouped into four speech families.

The languages used in the north are very different from the languages of the south, but most people know at least one of the official languages. English, which is understood by many, is widely used as the language for government and business.

Women wash themselves and their clothes in a river. India's great rivers play a major part in most people's daily and religious lives. ▼

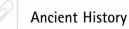
The Indus Valley civilization that developed in the north of India and the Dravidian culture that formed in central and southern India were two of the oldest known cultures in Asia. The Indus Valley civilization flourished for nearly 1,000 years beginning around 2500 B.C. Dravidians were thought to be descendants of the Indus Valley civilization that were pushed south by invading Aryans in around 1500 B.C.

◀◀ People at a street market in Orissa state, east India. The market has been set up outside a Hindu temple.

Web Search ▶▶

▶ **www.censusindia.net**
Discover facts and figures about India's population from the latest national census.

▶ **www.nic.in**
General facts and figures from the country's National Information Center.

▶ **www.mapsofindia.com**
Study a variety of maps of India.

▶ **www.indianmuseum-calcutta.org**
Discover the traditions, customs, and handicrafts of India's people over the ages at this museum's site.

Urban and Rural Life

The difference between urban and rural life in India is often striking. Cities offer the latest in technology, whereas electricity has only recently become available in some villages. Metropolitan cities can also be very overcrowded.

Most Indians live in villages and small towns, but more and more young people are moving to the cities in search of jobs and the attractions of modern city life.

Houses with servants

Standards of living vary greatly depending on where a person lives and how wealthy they are. Rich families in cities might live in large homes surrounded by high walls and a gate, and have several servants. Employing servants is almost considered a social duty because it gives jobs to poorer families. A middle-class family might live in a

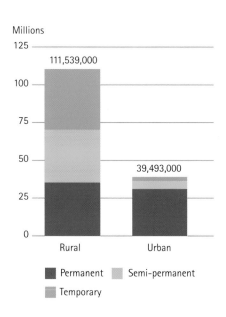

Millions

- 111,539,000 (Rural)
- 39,493,000 (Urban)

Permanent Semi-permanent
Temporary

▲ Numbers of different types of homes.

In rural areas, most people work on the land, often using animals to pull plows and turn grindstones. ▼

small apartment in a larger building or in a small house. City houses are usually made of cement or brick with roofs of tile, slate, wood, or corrugated iron. There are indoor plumbing facilities, although in some apartment buildings families share a bathroom.

Mud and straw buildings

In the villages there are also differences between rich and poor. Families that are well-off may have two-story brick houses with electricity and running water. Poor villagers have small houses made of mud and straw or planks of wood and palm leaves. Not all villages have electricity. Many village homes have no indoor plumbing. Drinking water is carried from village wells, and people bathe in nearby lakes or streams.

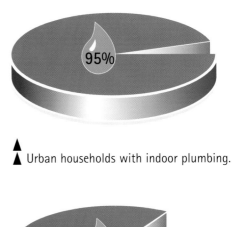

▲ Urban households with indoor plumbing.

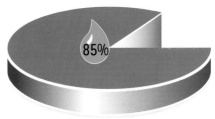

▲ Rural households with indoor plumbing.

In big cities such as Mumbai, poor people live in slums in shelters made of cardboard and sheets of iron. ▼▼

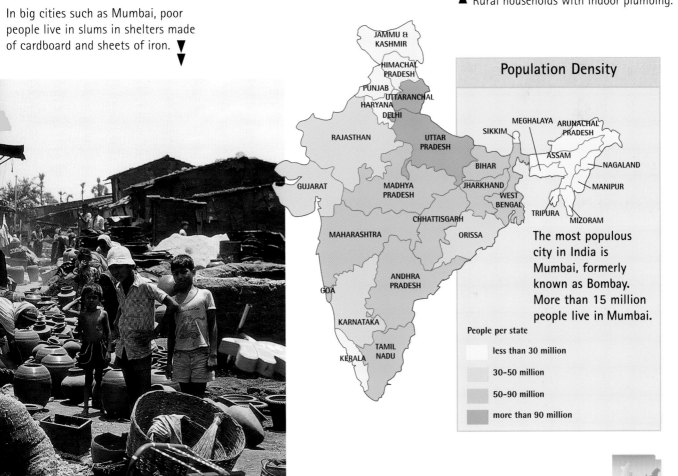

JAMMU & KASHMIR
HIMACHAL PRADESH
PUNJAB
UTTARANCHAL
HARYANA
DELHI
RAJASTHAN
UTTAR PRADESH
SIKKIM
MEGHALAYA
ARUNACHAL PRADESH
ASSAM
NAGALAND
BIHAR
GUJARAT
MADHYA PRADESH
JHARKHAND
WEST BENGAL
MANIPUR
TRIPURA
MIZORAM
CHHATTISGARH
MAHARASHTRA
ORISSA
GOA
ANDHRA PRADESH
KARNATAKA
TAMIL NADU
KERALA

Population Density

The most populous city in India is Mumbai, formerly known as Bombay. More than 15 million people live in Mumbai.

People per state

	less than 30 million
	30–50 million
	50–90 million
	more than 90 million

Farming Regions

New Delhi

The main farming regions are in the northeast and south.

protected wildlife areas

tea

root crops

rice

fruit

fish

cotton

forest and woodland

grassland and pasture

non-agricultural and desert

On tea plantations in Darjeeling, northern India, tea leaves are collected by hand.

Local fishermen bring in their catch on a beach in Kerala. India has six major and many smaller fishing harbors. ▼

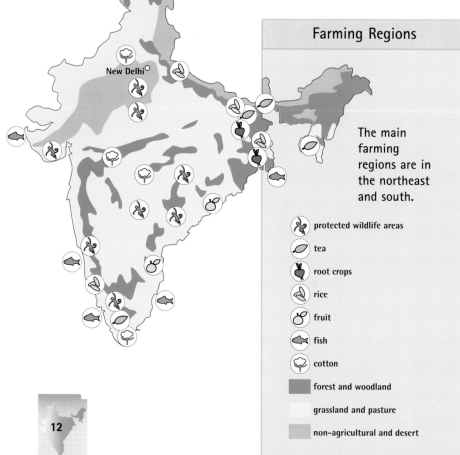

Farming and Fishing

The farming industry in India employs over half the population. India is one of the world's largest producers of milk, sugar cane, and fruit. Fishing is also important because of India's long coastline, and employs about one million people.

Most farms in India occupy less than three acres (1 h). More now use irrigation to lessen their dependence on the monsoon rains. Other recent advances in farming include the increased use of fertilizers and pesticides.

The growing seasons

Rice, millet, cotton, and jute are planted between May and July and harvested from September to October. Wheat, barley, oilseeds, and pulses (legumes) are planted during October and November and harvested from February to April. Sugarcane takes 10 to 18 months to mature and is planted at various times of the year.

Many vegetables, spices, and fruits are grown and sold locally. The food processing industry is expanding. India produces crackers, chocolate and cocoa butter, pasta, condensed milk, and soft drinks. It grows rubber trees from which latex, the source of rubber, is harvested as it runs out of the bark.

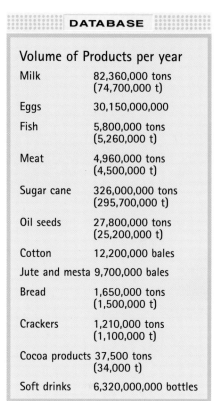

DATABASE	
Volume of Products per year	
Milk	82,360,000 tons (74,700,000 t)
Eggs	30,150,000,000
Fish	5,800,000 tons (5,260,000 t)
Meat	4,960,000 tons (4,500,000 t)
Sugar cane	326,000,000 tons (295,700,000 t)
Oil seeds	27,800,000 tons (25,200,000 t)
Cotton	12,200,000 bales
Jute and mesta	9,700,000 bales
Bread	1,650,000 tons (1,500,000 t)
Crackers	1,210,000 tons (1,100,000 t)
Cocoa products	37,500 tons (34,000 t)
Soft drinks	6,320,000,000 bottles

Fishing

India is the sixth largest producer of fish in the world. Fish are canned and frozen mostly for the export market. Fish and fish byproducts are used to make gelatin and glue, while ground, dried fish is used to feed chickens.

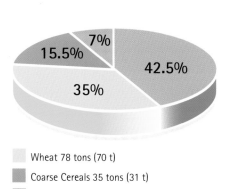

Wheat 78 tons (70 t)

Coarse Cereals 35 tons (31 t)

Pulses 16 tons (14 t)

Rice 95 tons (86 t)

▲ Grain production. Rice is the most important crop.

Resources and Industry

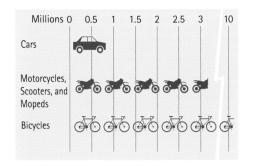

Manufacture of vehicles per year.

India is rich in many minerals, especially in the peninsula region. The country is making increased use of its mineral resources while at the same time developing modern, high-technology industries.

India has exploited its mineral resources for thousands of years. There are records of mining in Rajasthan from 1260–160 B.C. Today, India's largest mineral resource is coal. It is estimated there are over 231 billion tons (210 billion t) in the ground. This is enough coal to last India 100 more years at the rate it is currently being mined.

India is also the world's largest producer of mica, which is used in wafer-thin slices as an electrical or heat insulator. India's other mineral resources include iron ore, bauxite (from which aluminium is extracted), lignite, crude oil, natural gas, diamonds, and limestone.

The major mining and industrial areas are in Bihar in the northeast, in Madhya Pradesh in central India, and in Karnataka in the south.

Energy

India's demand for energy has increased steadily over the last 50 years. All urban centers and 85 percent of villages have access to electricity. Most power is generated from coal in thermal power plants, but India also has hydroelectric and nuclear power plants.

However, the demand for electricity has consistently been greater than the amount produced, so power blackouts are still common in many parts of the country. In some rural areas, firewood, agricultural waste, and cow dung are still burned as fuels. These fuels are collected by villagers by hand from nearby fields or forests.

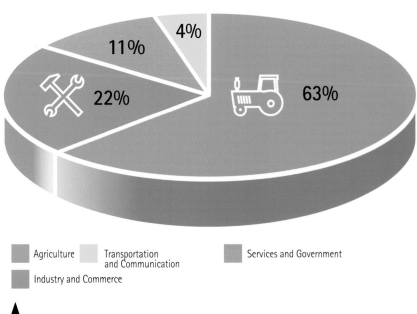

Agriculture   Transportation and Communication   Services and Government

Industry and Commerce

Proportion of workers in major industries.

Industries and products

The textile industry employs around 20 million people who make yarn, woven and knitted fabrics, clothing, industrial and household textiles, silk, carpets, and jute. Preparing diamonds and other precious gems and stones for export is also an important industry.

Other industries gaining importance in India are the steel industry, cement production, leather industry, automobile manufacturing, food processing, software industry, and electronics manufacturing.

 Tamil Nadu in southern India is rich in forests, which are exploited for timber.

Product volumes per year.

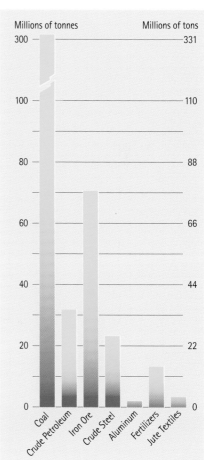

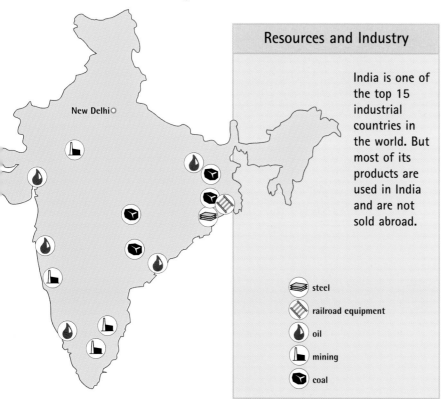

Resources and Industry

India is one of the top 15 industrial countries in the world. But most of its products are used in India and are not sold abroad.

- 🖺 steel
- ▨ railroad equipment
- ⬤ oil
- 🏭 mining
- ◐ coal

Transportation

Trains and long-distance buses are still the most popular ways to travel in India, but the use of cars is increasing, and the country is working to improve its already crowded roads. Air travel within India is slowly developing.

India's road network, the second largest in the world, has over 2,050,000 miles (3,300,000 km) of roads. Many main roads have only single lanes, so they can be very crowded and chaotic, especially around major cities. Drivers are supposed to drive on the left, but most rules of the road are loosely observed.

The number of motor vehicles using the roads increases by nearly 10 percent each year. The government is planning to build expressways and to widen and strengthen existing highways to improve road travel.

Indian Railways

India's railroad is the second largest singly–operated rail network in the world, with 38,985 miles (62,725 km) of track.

Every day Indian Railways carries 12 million people and over a million tons of freight.

Railway workers repair tracks at Jaisalmer in Rajasthan. ▼

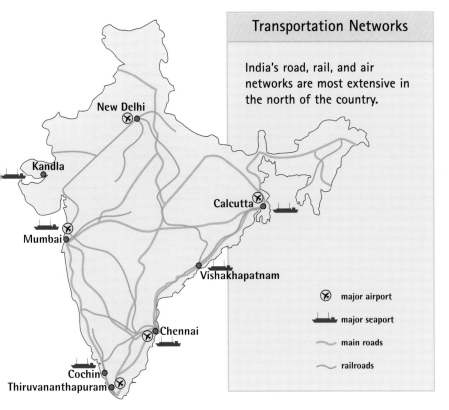

Transportation Networks

India's road, rail, and air networks are most extensive in the north of the country.

 major airport

major seaport

main roads

railroads

Urban Transportation

In all major cities and towns, public transportation is available in the form of buses, trains, trolleys, taxis, and auto-rickshaws.

Only Calcutta has an underground railway, but work has started on the New Delhi Metro, with plans to open it in 2005.

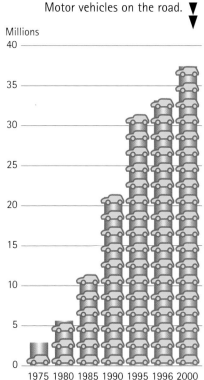

Motor vehicles on the road. ▼▼

Millions

40

35

30

25

20

15

10

5

0

1975 1980 1985 1990 1995 1996 2000

Ships

In the states of Kerala and West Bengal, inland river transportation—barges, ships, and ferries on rivers and canals—is used to move people, farm animals, and goods from one place to another.

India has a large shipping fleet, with numerous ocean-going oil tankers and cargo ships and hundreds of smaller coastal vessels. No regular passenger ships operate to India, although some world cruise ships do make stops at ports of interest to tourists such as Mumbai, Marmagao, Cochin, and Chennai.

Air travel

Air networks using about 350 national airports connect cities within India. There are several flights a day between such cities as New Delhi, Mumbai, Calcutta, and Madras. Numerous international air routes connect India to major cities in Europe and Asia. Most international flights land in New Delhi or Mumbai, but there are several other international airports in the country.

Web Search ►►

► www.mapsofindia.com/distances

This site will tell you the distance by road between many cities and even map out a travel route for you.

► www.indian.rail.gov.in

Schedules and train information for India's rail network.

17

Education

I ndia has made great progress in increasing its levels of education. By 2000, the literacy rate had risen to 58 percent from only 18 percent in 1951.

Free education is available at government schools to all children between the ages of 6 and 14. About 92 percent of children attend elementary school, but only 57 percent attend middle school, which is for children aged 11 to 14.

Many poor families send their older children to work rather than let them go to school. In addition, many more boys than girls attend middle school because women in India are still expected to stay at home and look after children. Children in government schools get a free meal at noon to help persuade their families to send them there.

Private schools and universities

Children in cities often have the option of going to private school, which their parents must pay for. Private schools have better teachers and better equipment than the free government schools. Children from private schools are more likely to go on to a university. Often students will travel to other countries for their higher education, but there are many colleges and universities in India.

Number of primary school pupils. ▼▼

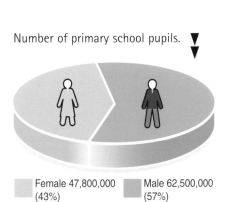

Female 47,800,000 (43%) Male 62,500,000 (57%)

Number of middle school pupils. ▼▼

Female 16,300,000 (39.7%) Male 24,700,000 (60.3%)

Number of secondary school pupils. ▼▼

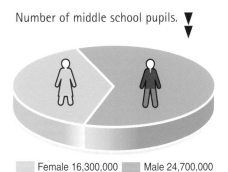

Female 9,700,000 (36%) Male 17,200,000 (64%)

►► Adult classes teach women to read and write.

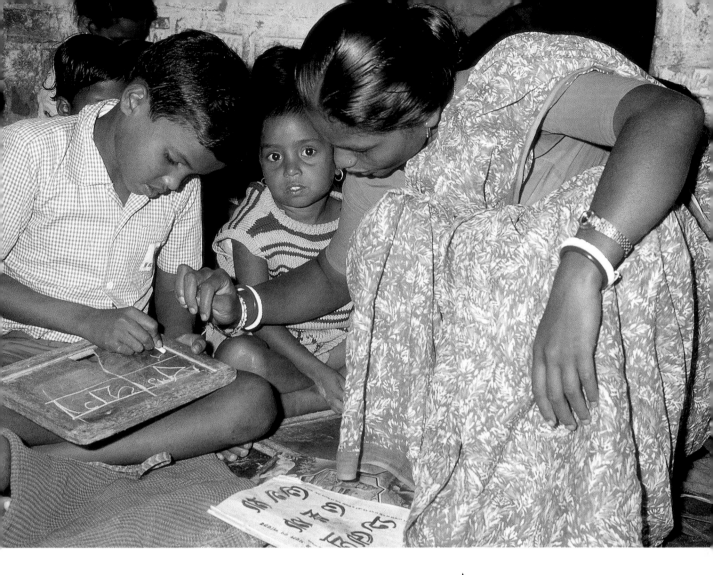

The school day begins at 9:00 a.m. and finishes at 3:30 p.m., with short breaks and a longer lunch break at 1:00 p.m. Classes can include a native language, English, math, science, art, social studies, physical education, geography, and history.

▲ Many village schools cannot afford writing paper and pens. Children use chalk to write on slate boards.

◄◄ Numbers of men and women attending a university in India.

| 0 | 1.0 | 2.0 | 3.0 | 4.0 Millions |

Web Search ▶▶

▶ www.goidirectory.nic.in
Go to this directory of Government of India websites for more information about education.

Sports and Leisure

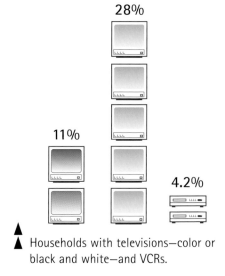

28%

11%

4.2%

▲ Households with televisions—color or black and white—and VCRs.

M any sports are played throughout India. Polo, as it is played today, spread around the world from India just over a hundred years ago. There are also many other traditional Indian games. Squash, tennis, badminton, and cricket—brought to India by British colonists—are now extremely popular.

Hockey

Field hockey is the national game of India. From 1928 to 1956 India won six consecutive Olympic gold medals, and the country has won eight Olympic hockey gold medals in total. Today, organized hockey is played at university level to encourage the development of world-class hockey talent.

Games of cricket are being played in this recreation park in Calcutta. ▼

Cricket

India loves cricket. Children play cricket in streets and parks, and almost everyone seems to stop to watch or listen to important matches on TV or the radio. There are many stadiums throughout India where cricket matches are held. India has won the cricket World Cup twice, in 1987 and again in 1996.

Other sports

In 1982 New Delhi built modern sports facilities in order to host the ninth Asian Games. Other sports played in India include archery, billiards, swimming, chess, judo, table tennis, tennis, and golf. There are also camel races and elephant races, unique to India.

Leisure activities for the wealthy include going to plays or movies. Poorer people cannot always afford these entertainments. Instead, they watch television. Not everyone in India owns a television, but they often watch programs by gathering at the house of someone who does.

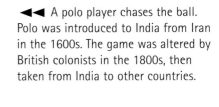

◄◄ A polo player chases the ball. Polo was introduced to India from Iran in the 1600s. The game was altered by British colonists in the 1800s, then taken from India to other countries.

▲ A Hindu holy man and a tourist ride on an Indian elephant through the streets of Udaipur, Rajasthan, as part of a religious celebration.

►► Hindu holy men meditate on the banks of the Ganges at Varanasi, also known as Benares or Kashi. Hindus believe in washing in the sacred waters of the Ganges to get rid of evil forces.

Daily Life and Religion

Religion is at the center of people's way of life in India. The main religions are Hinduism, Islam, Buddhism, and Sikhism. Temples, holy sites, holy rivers, and religious icons and images are everywhere.

Many Hindus worship at a shrine in their home dedicated to one of the Hindu gods. They also make long journeys to visit holy places in India. Hindus believe in the idea that there are four types of people (or castes). Many Hindus do not like to mix with anyone from a lower caste. Discrimination on the basis of caste is now illegal in India, but peoples' attitudes are difficult to change.

Among other religious groups, Muslims, who are followers of Islam, pray five times each day. Sikh males generally wear colored turbans on their heads and have long beards because they do not cut their hair. Most Jains, believers in strict respect for all life, are vegetarian and cover their mouths to avoid swallowing germs or insects.

Shopping

Modern shopping malls are found in the largest cities, but bazaars, or local markets full of open-air stalls, are more commonplace. They include candy stores, bookstores, and toy stores. At markets and private shops people bargain for the price of what they buy. However, the government operates special shops in cities where prices are fixed.

Armed forces

India has an army, a navy, an air force, and a coast guard. In addition to military operations, the forces provide assistance during times of flood or earthquake. Enlistment in the armed forces is voluntary and open to all Indian citizens 17 years or older, although most soldiers are male. Recently, the government allowed women officers in a few non-combat areas.

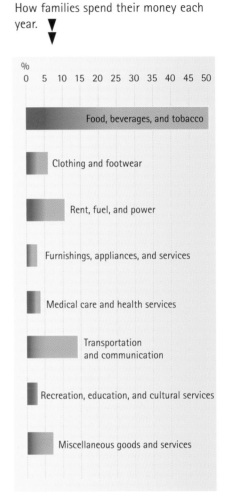

How families spend their money each year.

- Food, beverages, and tobacco
- Clothing and footwear
- Rent, fuel, and power
- Furnishings, appliances, and services
- Medical care and health services
- Transportation and communication
- Recreation, education, and cultural services
- Miscellaneous goods and services

Web Search ►►

► **www.nic.in**
Facts and figures about religion and the armed forces from the National Information Center.

► **www.indiaserver.com.**
News stories from the national website.

Arts and Media

Music, theater, the visual arts, and literature all have their place in modern Indian society. So, too, do newspapers, magazines, and television. Indian movies are world famous for their rich variety.

Today, museums and galleries are found in most larger cities. The museums of national importance are the National Museum in New Delhi, the Indian Museum in Calcutta, and the Salarjang Museum in Hyderabad. There are two National Galleries of Modern Art and 26 science centers and museums operated by the government.

All India Radio (AIR) is broadcast on 198 radio stations. Public service television in India reaches nearly 90 percent of the population. An estimated 69 million homes have television sets. In addition to the national network, many Indians can now watch satellite and cable TV. Most newspapers in India are published in Hindi, but newspapers are also published in about 100 other languages and dialects.

A concert hall in Madras. ▼▼

Overseas visitors

Tourism is a relatively new industry in India, only gaining popularity in the 1980s. India promotes its cultural heritage and many colorful fairs and festivals to tourists. In 2000, the total foreign tourist traffic to India was about 2.5 million people. The most popular attraction is the Taj Mahal, the tomb of an empress who died in 1631.

Bollywood

More films are made in India (over 900 annually) than in Hollywood, California, or anywhere else in the world. Movie theaters are almost everywhere, and watching movies is very popular—but poor people cannot always afford to go.

The city of Mumbai (once known as Bombay) is nicknamed Bollywood because it is the center of the Indian movie industry.

 A billboard for a "Bollywood" film.

Web Search ▶▶

▶ www.webindia.com
Traditional music, crafts, and dance

▶ www.ddindia.com
Watch Doordarshan TV station

▶ www.timesofindia.com
One of India's national newspapers

▶ www.hinduonline.com
The Hindu newspaper site

Government

From 1858 until independence in 1947, India was governed by Great Britain. The modern Republic of India founded in 1947 is a democracy modeled after the British parliamentary system. The country's leaders are the president, vice president, and a council of ministers that is headed by the prime minister.

Each of India's states has a governing assembly, and in some cases even a second chamber, which is elected by the people of that state. The head of each state is called a governor and is formally appointed by the president of India. The Union Territories are governed by the president through an appointed administrator.

India Gate, a World War I memorial, near the Presidential Palace in New Delhi, the capital city of India.

Government House in Bangalore, the capital city of the state of Karnataka. ▼

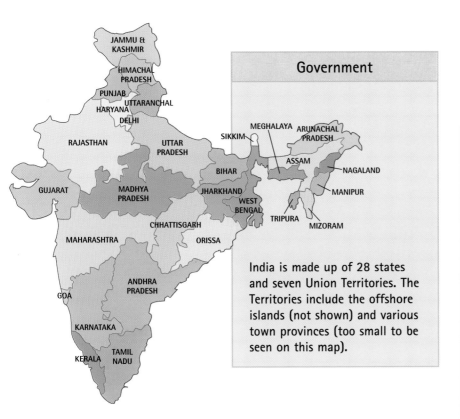

Government

India is made up of 28 states and seven Union Territories. The Territories include the offshore islands (not shown) and various town provinces (too small to be seen on this map).

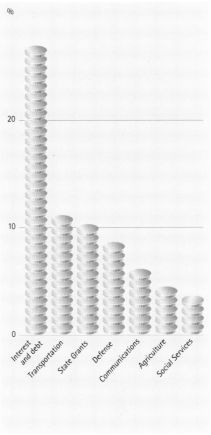

How the Indian government spends money each year. ▼

The President

The House of the People, or the Lok Sabha, has up to 552 members, of which 550 are directly elected by the people. The Council of States, or Rajya Sabha, is made up of no more than 250 members elected by members of the different states' governments. India's president is the head of state and commander-in-chief of the armed forces. Presidents are elected by members of both houses of parliament and members of the states' legislatures.

The prime minister

The prime minister is formally appointed by the president and is the leader of the political party that wins the most votes in a general election. The prime minister and the council of ministers have the real authority to make decisions in the country.

India is a secular country, guaranteeing the freedom of religious beliefs. All Indian citizens, once they have reached the age of 18, are able to vote.

Web Search ▶▶

▶ www.indiabudget.nic.in
For all the latest government budget information

▶ www.goidirectory.nic.in
The directory of Government of India websites

▶ www.pib.nic.in
India's Press Information Bureau

Place in the World

DATABASE

Chronology of Historical Events up to A.D. 1600

8500–2500 B.C. Agricultural settlements in the general area of the Indus Valley

2000 B.C. Indus Valley civilization disappears

1500 B.C. Vedic period, when Aryan settlers move in; civilization concentrated between the Ganges and Yamuna Rivers

1200–500 B.C. Emergence of Hindu religion; early Hindu religious texts are written

570–450 B.C. Spread of Buddhism and Jainism

326 B.C. Alexander the Great invades northwest India

320–232 B.C. Mauryan Dynasty dominates most of India

185 B.C.–A.D. 300 Smaller kingdoms trade with each other and with Greece and Rome

A.D. 319–467 Gupta Empire, classical age of Indian art and sculpture; trade with Arabia, China, Southeast Asia

600–1192 Regional kingdoms dominate

1206 Islamic dynasty; various sultans rule

1526-1707 Mughal Empire; Emperors Babur, Humayun, Akbar, Jahangir, Shah Jahan, Aurangzeb rule in succession

1469-1538 Rise of Sikhism

1498 Vasco da Gama reaches India

1542 St. Francis Xavier, first Christian missionary, arrives

Although the civilizations of India are thousands of years old, the modern Republic of India is a young nation that is still developing, both at home and in the world at large. The country's large and fast-growing population creates great demands on its resources, but India is famous the world over for the richness and vitality of its culture.

India is working to reduce its illiteracy rates, eliminate energy shortages, create a widespread telecommunications system, and improve its road, rail, and air networks. This will increase national prosperity and the importance of the part India already plays on the world stage.

International links and political changes

India takes part in many international organizations, including the United Nations, UNESCO, the World Health Organization, and Interpol. It is also a member of cooperative organizations in Asia, which work together to create economic benefits, solve security and border issues, and help with social issues such as poverty.

India's recent history has been dramatic. Two prime ministers have been assassinated: Indira Gandhi in 1984 and her son, Rajiv Gandhi, in 1991. Political corruption scandals arose in 1996, and a series of recent elections resulted in an increase in regional political parties.

During the 1990s the government's policies opened India to global trade and investment. This approach has continued, and India's economy continues to grow into the 21st century.

Chronology of Historical Events from A.D. 1600

1600 East India Company created by Queen Elizabeth I

1757 British East India Company gains control of Bengal and southeast India

1774 First British Governor General, Warren Hastings, takes charge

1857 British government takes control of India from the East India Company

1885 Indian National Congress is created

1906 Muslim League established

1920 Mahatma Gandhi leads the Indian National Congress party, begins non-violent campaign against British rule

1935 Great Britain passes Government of India Act to set plan for Indian self-government

1947 Muslim League demands a Muslim country separate from India

1947 August 15, independence from Great Britain; India joins the British Commonwealth as a dominion with Jawaharlal Nehru as Prime Minister. Pakistan, a Muslim country carved out of India, joins the Commonwealth a day earlier

1948 Gandhi is assassinated

1950 January 26, India becomes a republic within the Commonwealth after adopting its constitution

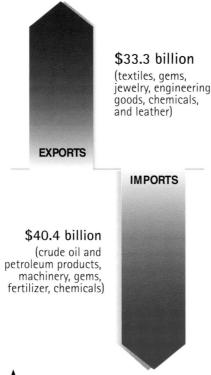

$33.3 billion
(textiles, gems, jewelry, engineering goods, chemicals, and leather)

EXPORTS

IMPORTS

$40.4 billion
(crude oil and petroleum products, machinery, gems, fertilizer, chemicals)

India's imports and exports.

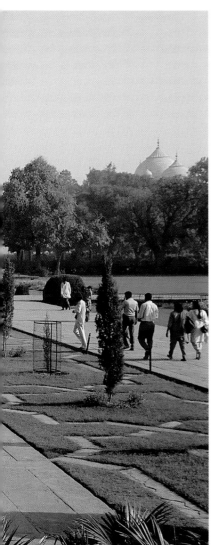

◄◄ The Taj Mahal, built between 1631 and 1648.

Area:
1,269,214 sq mi (3,287,263 sq km)

Population size:
846,300,000 (1991 Census);
1,000,100,000 (2000 estimate)

Capital city:
New Delhi

Other major cities:
Mumbai, Calcutta, Chennai,
Bangalore, Hyderabad, Ahmedabad

Longest Rivers:
Brahmaputra 1,802 miles (2,900 km),
Indus 1,802 miles (2,900 km),
Ganges 1,560 miles (2,510 km)

Highest mountain:
Kanchenjunga 28,209 ft (8,598 m)

Currency:
Indian rupees (Rs)
1 rupee=100 paise
US $1 = Rs 42.5 approximately

Flag:
Three horizontal bands: orange on
top, white in the middle, green on
the bottom. The white band has a
blue 24-spoked wheel (or chakra)
centered in it.

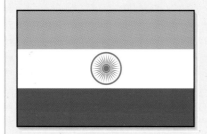

Languages:
18 official languages: Hindi,
Bengali, Telugu, Marathi, Tamil,
Urdu, Gujarati, Malayalam,
Kannada, Oriya, Punjabi, Assamese,
Sindhi, Kashmiri, Konkani, Nepali,
Manipuri, and Sanskrit; English is
commonly used and understood.

Major resources:
coal, mica, iron ore, bauxite,
lignite, aluminium, chromite,
manganese, titanium, crude oil,
natural gas, diamonds, and
limestone.

Major Exports:
textiles, gems and jewelry,
machinery, chemicals, leather,
marine products, rice, and tea.

**National holidays and major
events:**
January 26
Republic Day
May 1
May Day/Labor Day
August 15
Independence Day
October 2
Mahatma Gandhi's Birthday
December 25
Christmas Day

Religions:
India is officially secular; religions
practiced in the country include
Hinduism, Islam, Buddhism,
Jainism, Sikhism, Christianity,
Zoroastrianism, and Judaism

Glossary

AGRICULTURE
Farming the land, including plowing land, planting and raising crops, and raising animals.

BIRTH RATE
The number of babies born in a year compared to a set number of people.

CLIMATE
The type of weather a place has, including temperature, rainfall, and wind.

COMMONWEALTH
A voluntary, cooperative alliance of a group of nations linked by historical ties to Great Britain.

CONSUMER
A person that buys or uses goods and services.

CONTINENT
One of the seven largest landmasses in the world.

CULTURE
A group of people practicing the same traditions for many generations.

ECONOMY
The money earned by a country and/or the management of a country's earnings and expenses.

EXPORTS
Products, resources, or goods sold to other countries.

FERTILE
Land or soil that allows plants to grow easily and in large quantities.

GOVERNMENT
A group of people who manage a country, making laws, collecting taxes, and organizing health, education, transportation, and other systems.

GROSS DOMESTIC PRODUCT (GDP)
The value of products made by a country without subtracting the value of any debts owed by that country.

IMPORTS
Products, resources, or goods brought into the country.

IRRIGATION
Watering the land using artificial methods such as spraying, diverting streams, and flooding, in place of natural rainfall.

LITERACY
The ability to read and write.

MANUFACTURING
Making by hand or, more usually, by machine, a large quantity of something.

POPULATION
The number of people living in a defined area.

POPULATION DENSITY
The average number of people living in a specific land area, often given as per square mile or square kilometer.

RESOURCES
Materials that can be used to make goods, create energy, or generate money for a country or region.

RURAL
An area with low population; the countryside.

URBAN
Possessing the qualities of a city, such as a dense population housed in planned living zones.

Index